Sketches of Europe
(May-July 2012)

Stephen Alajajian

stephenalajajian@gmail.com

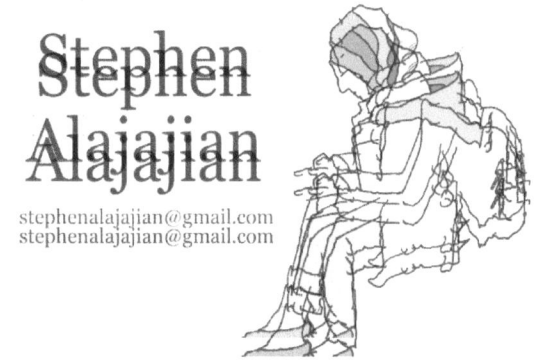

Published August 2019

Sketches of Europe
STEPHEN ALAJAJIAN

Valencia, Spain

San Sebastian, Spain

Paris, France

Poitiers, France

Toulouse, France

Valencia, Spain

San Sebastian, Spain

Paris, France

Poitiers, France

Toulouse, France

Dedicated to Dana Hurlbut

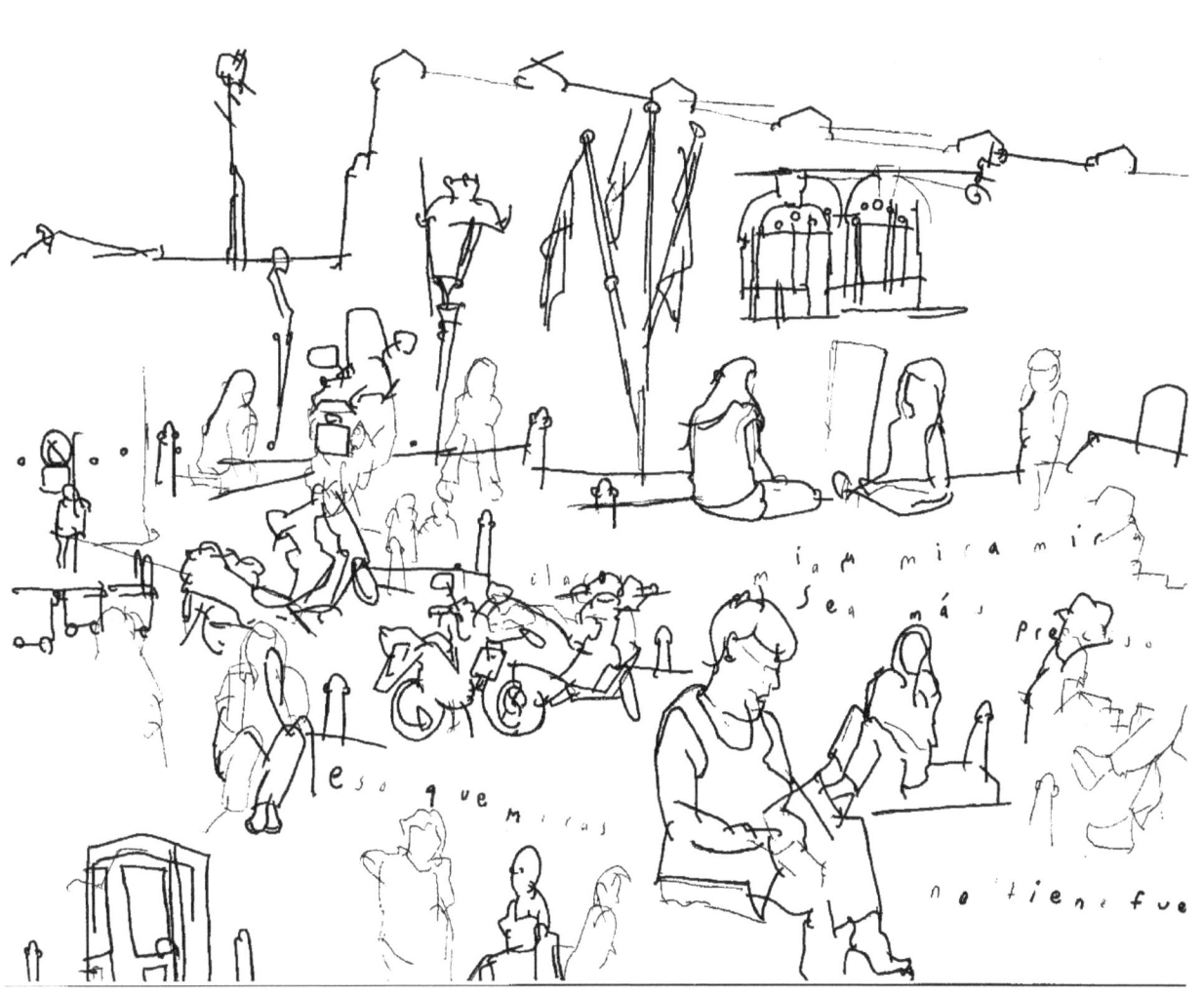

Untitled No. 1 (pen) / *Valencia, Spain*

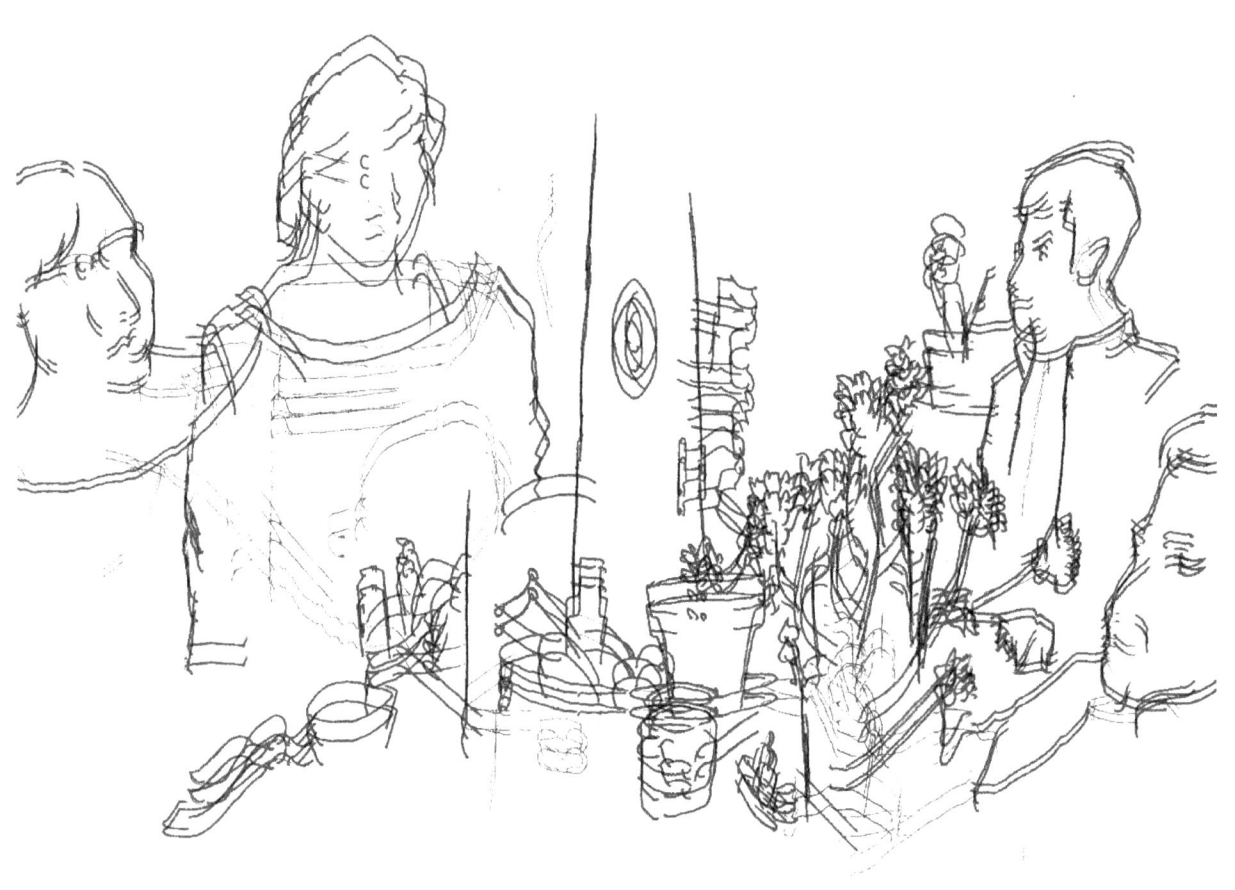

Becca and José (pen) / *Valencia, Spain*

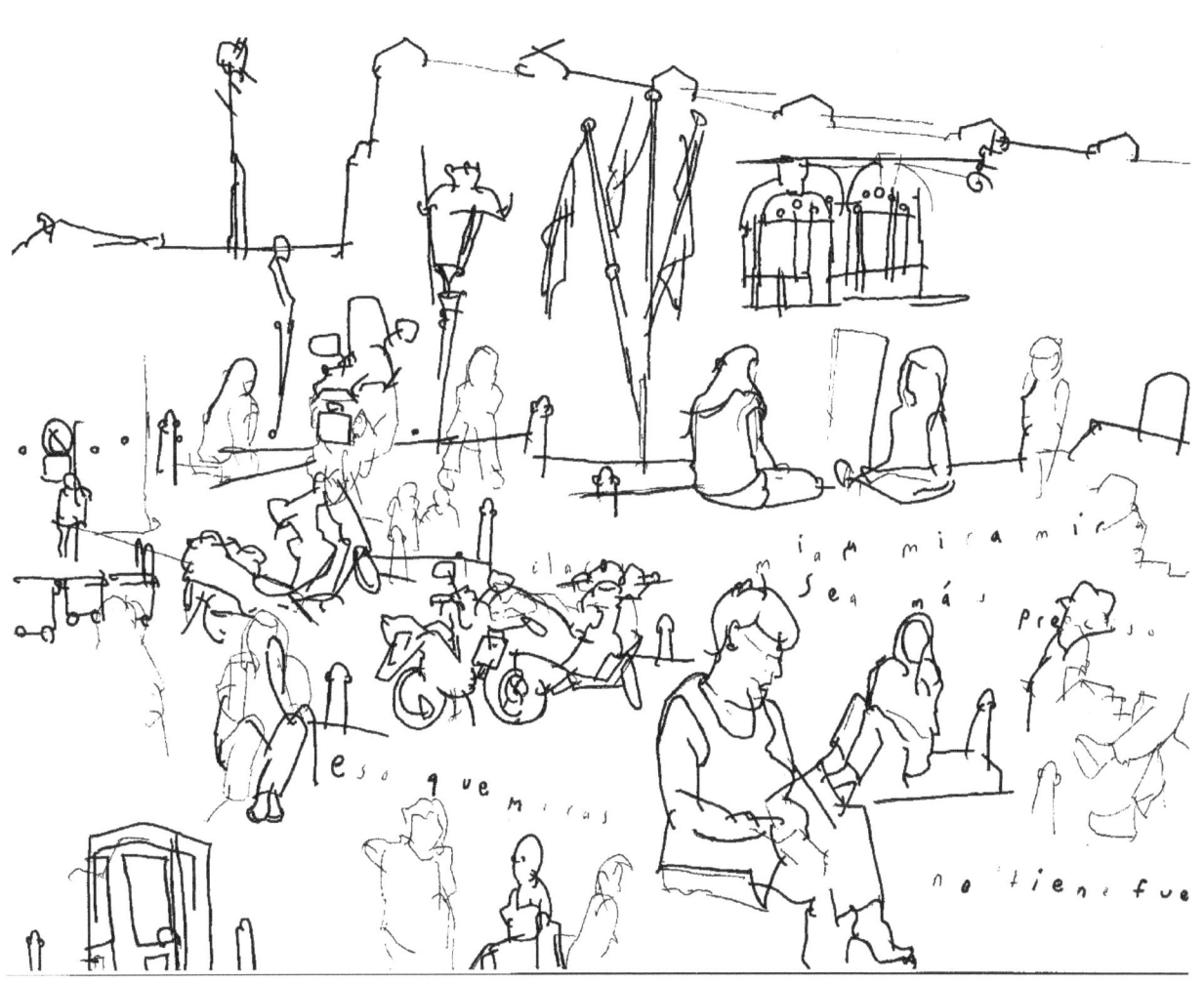

Untitled No. 1 (pen) / *Valencia, Spain*

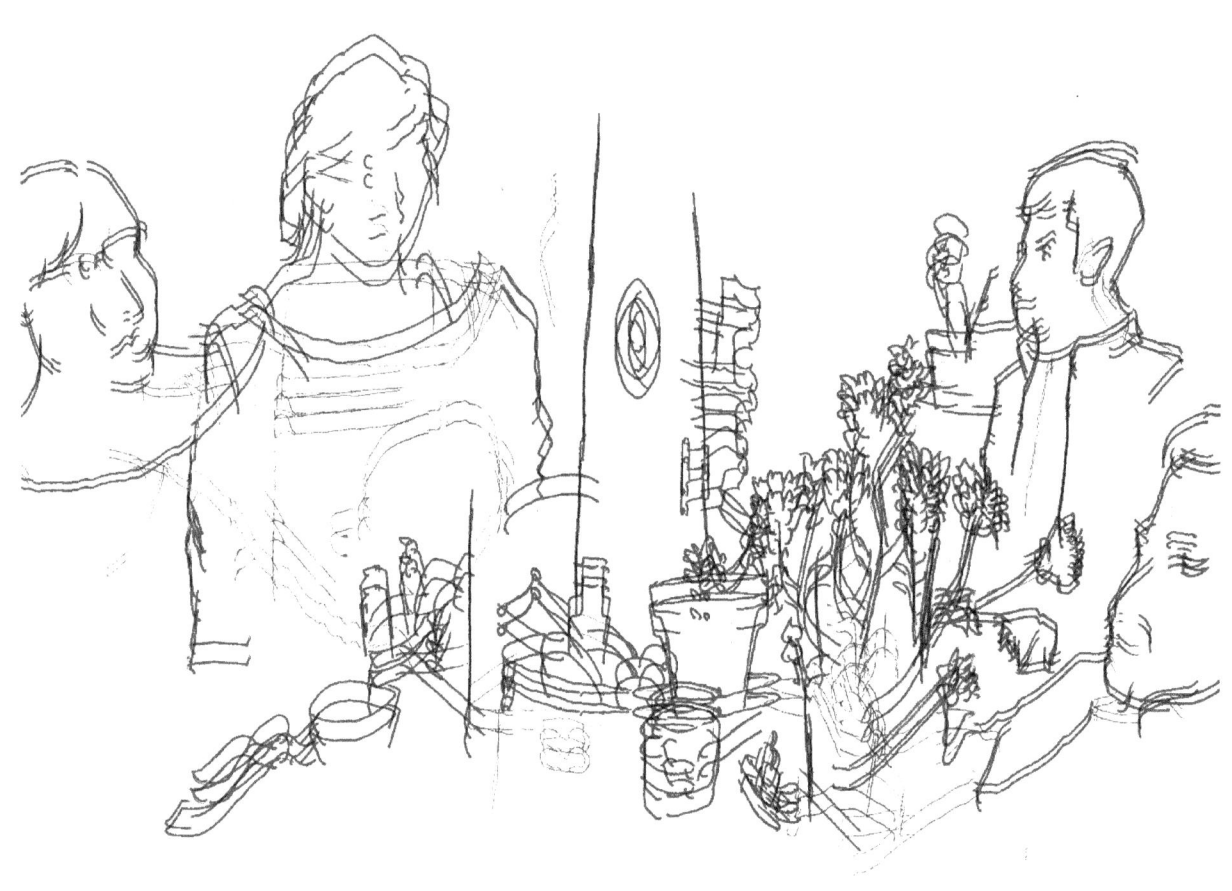

Becca and José (pen) / *Valencia, Spain*

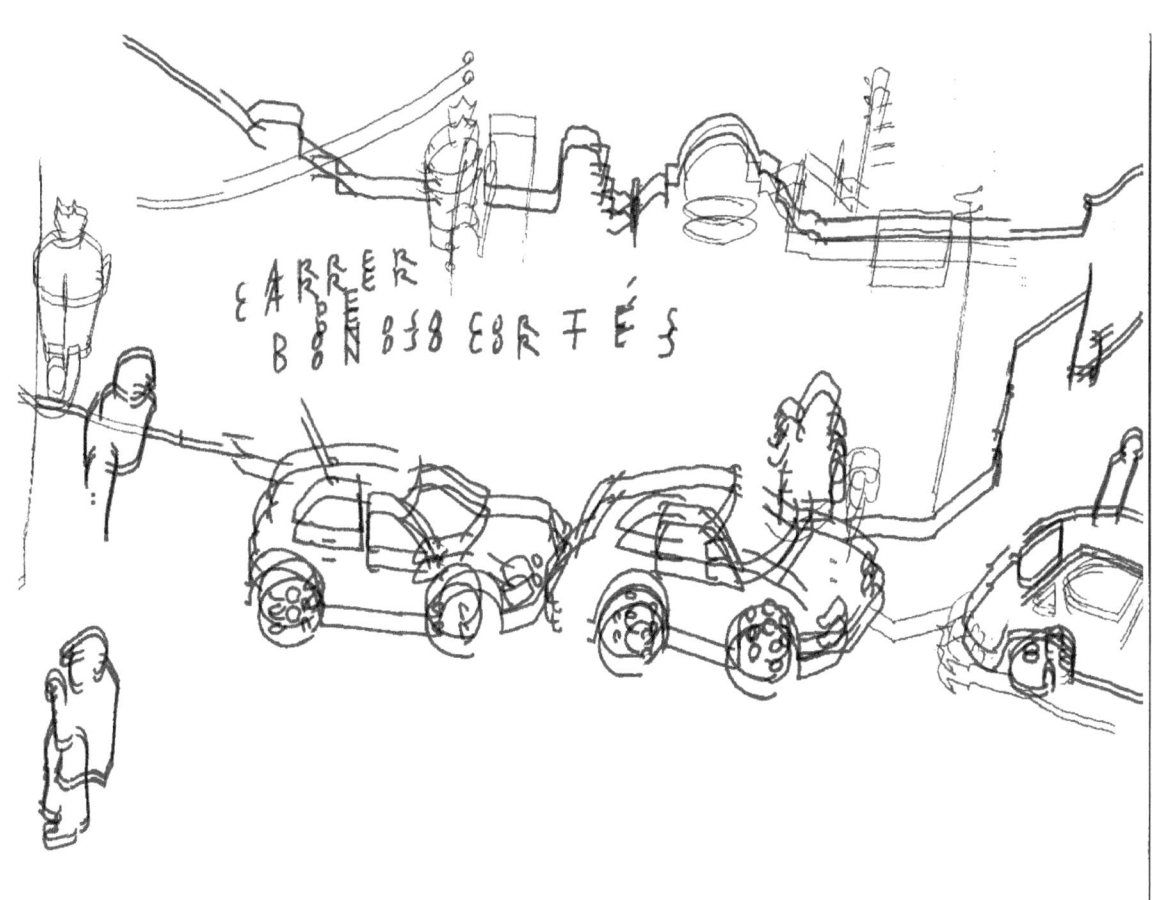

Calle de Donoso Cortés (pen) / *Valencia, Spain*

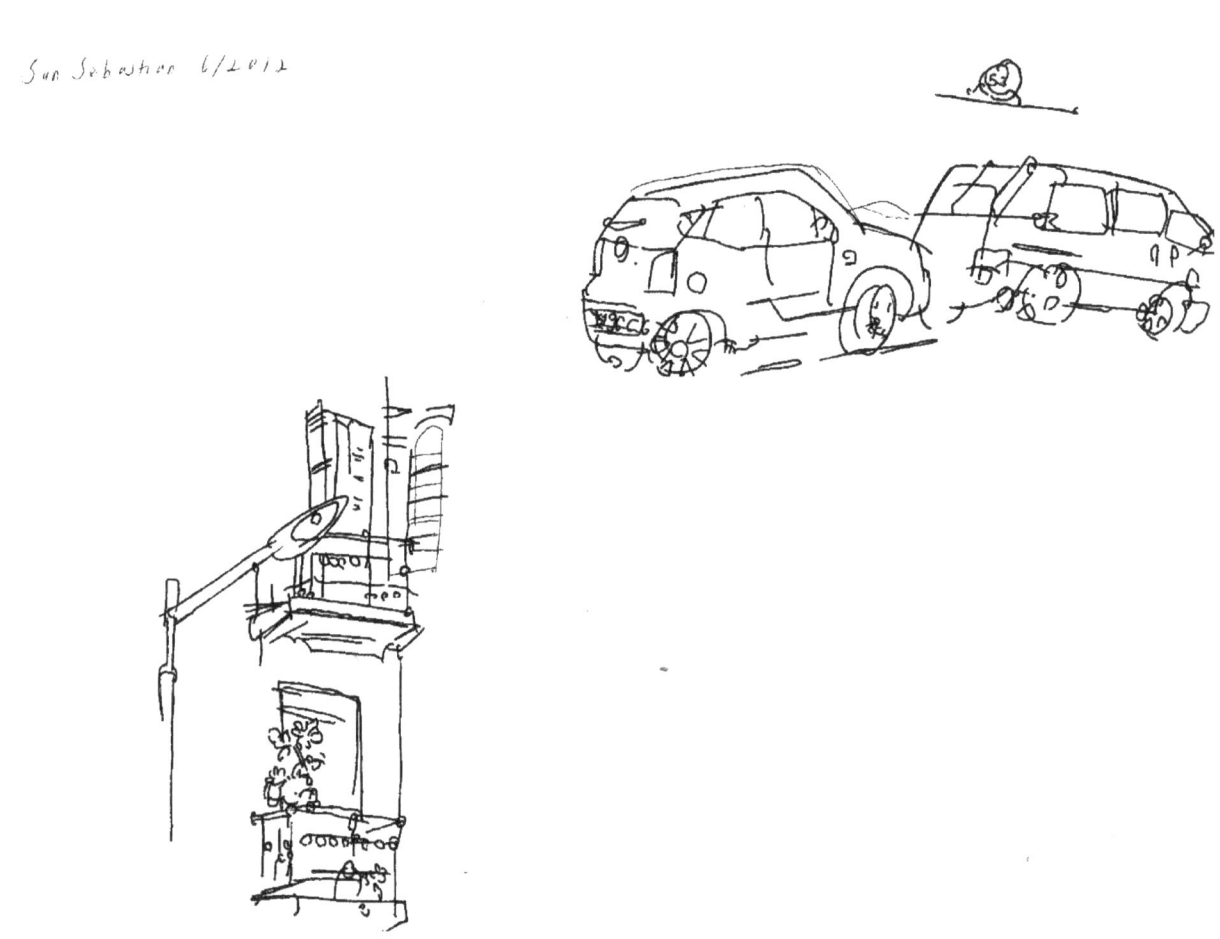

Untitled No. 1 (pen) / *San Sebastian, Spain*

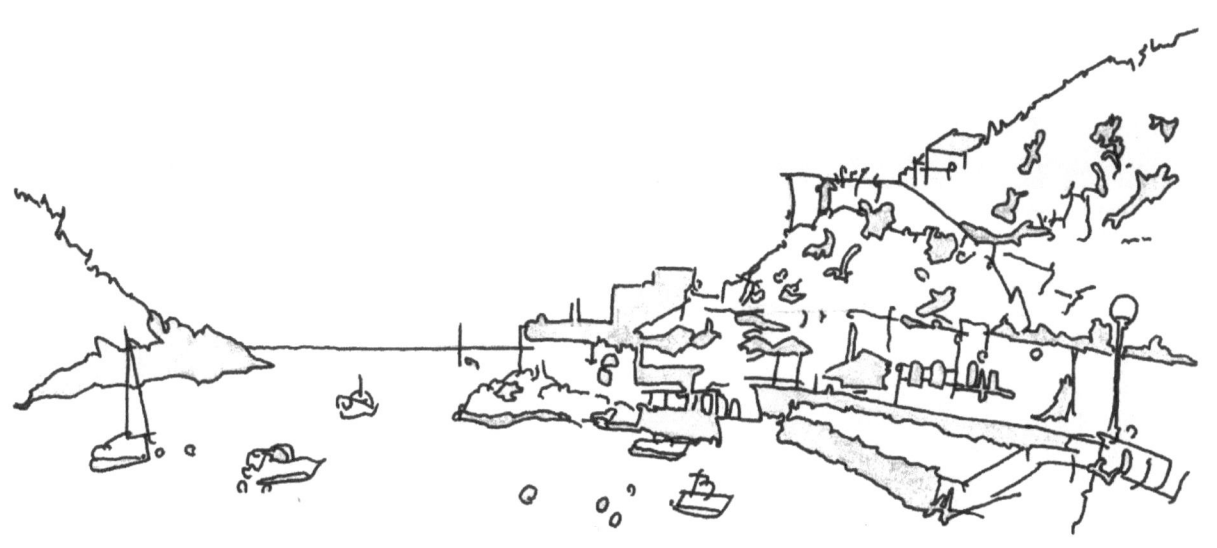

Untitled No. 2 (grayscale) / *San Sebastian, Spain*

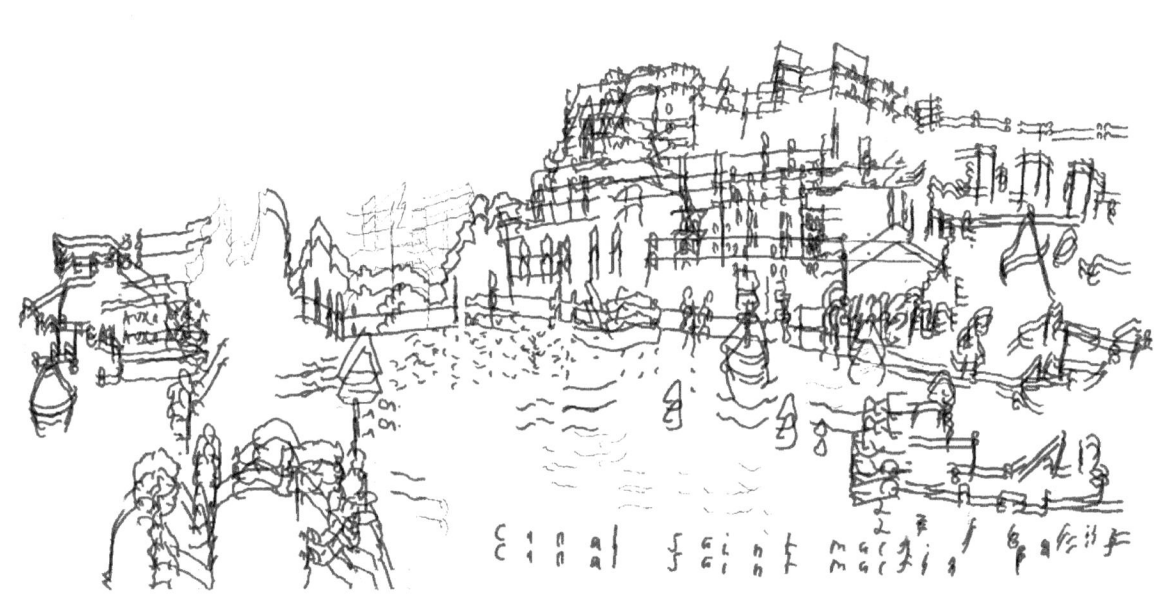

Canal Saint-Martin No. 1 (pen) / *Paris, France*

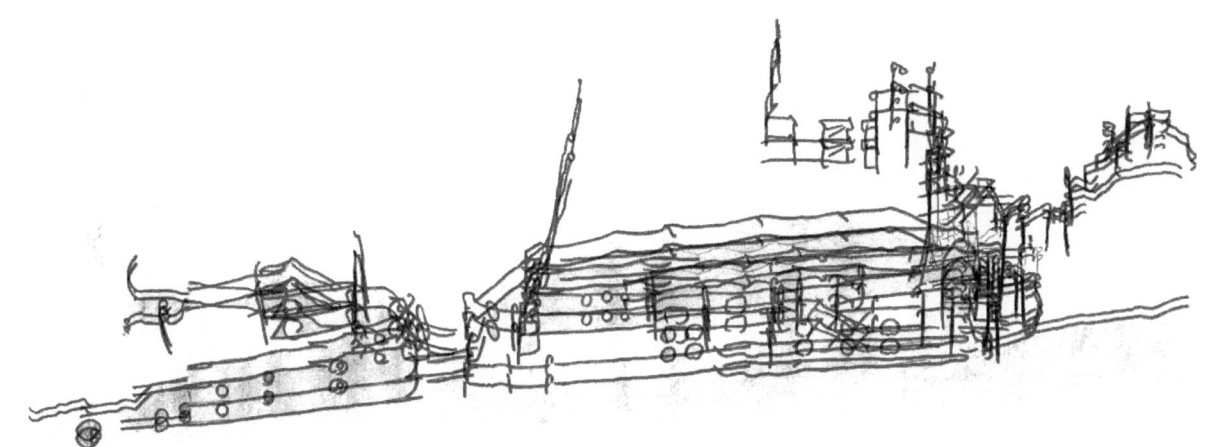

Canal Saint-Martin No: 2 (grayscale) / *Paris, France*

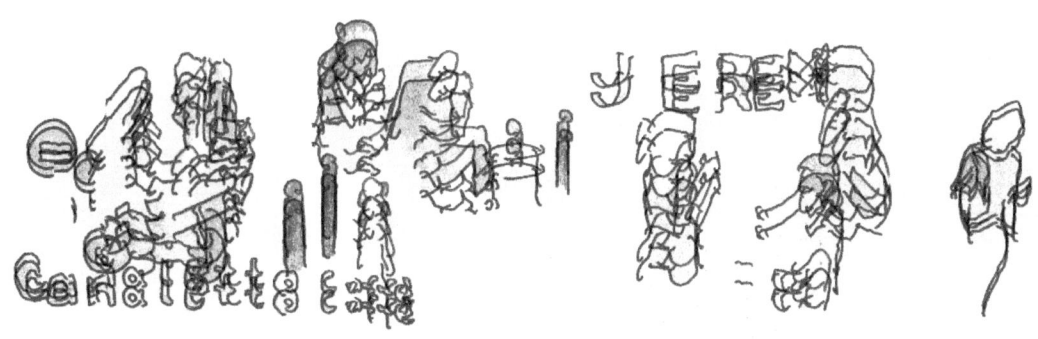

Canaletto Caffe (grayscale) / *Paris, France*

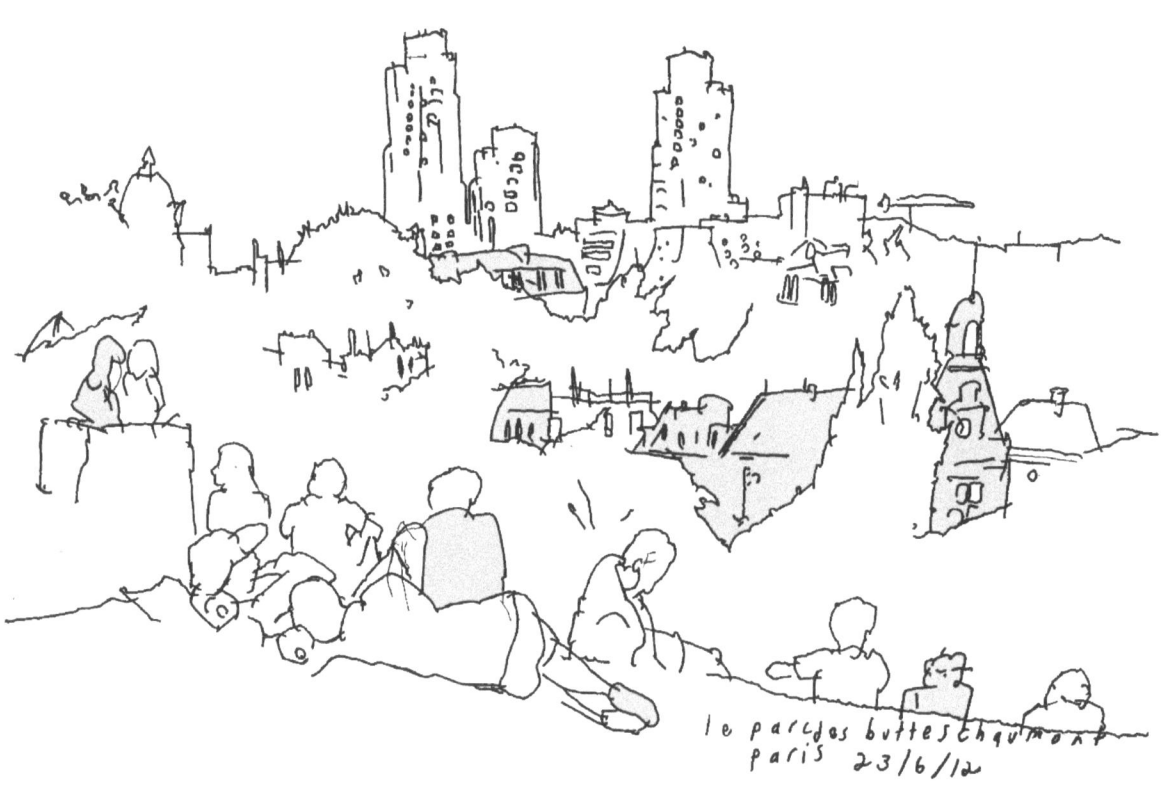

Le Parc des Buttes-Chaumont (pen w/ digital shading) / *Paris, France*

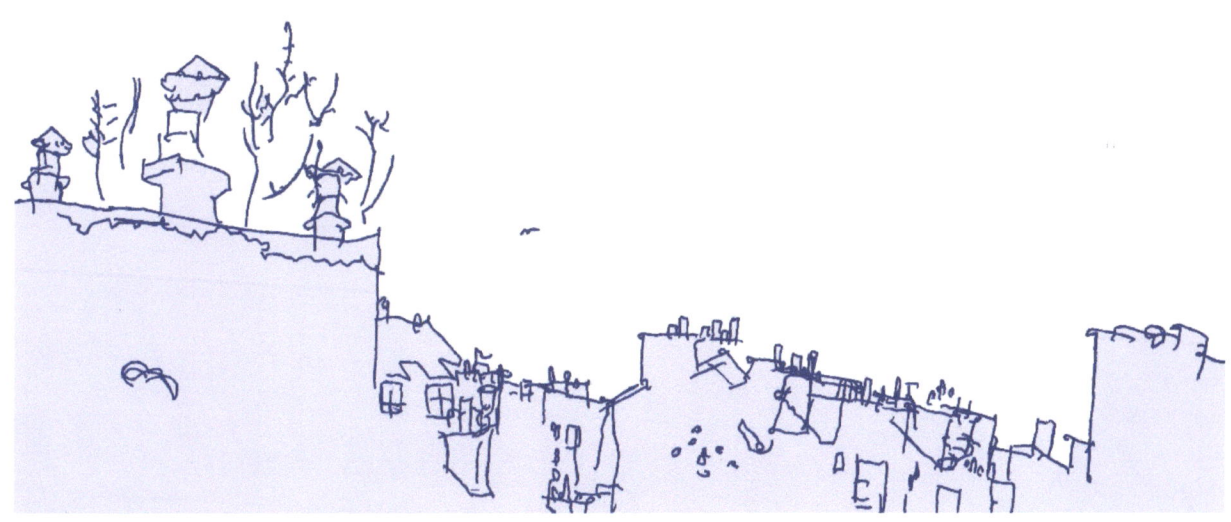

Rooftops (pen w/ digital color) / *Paris, France*

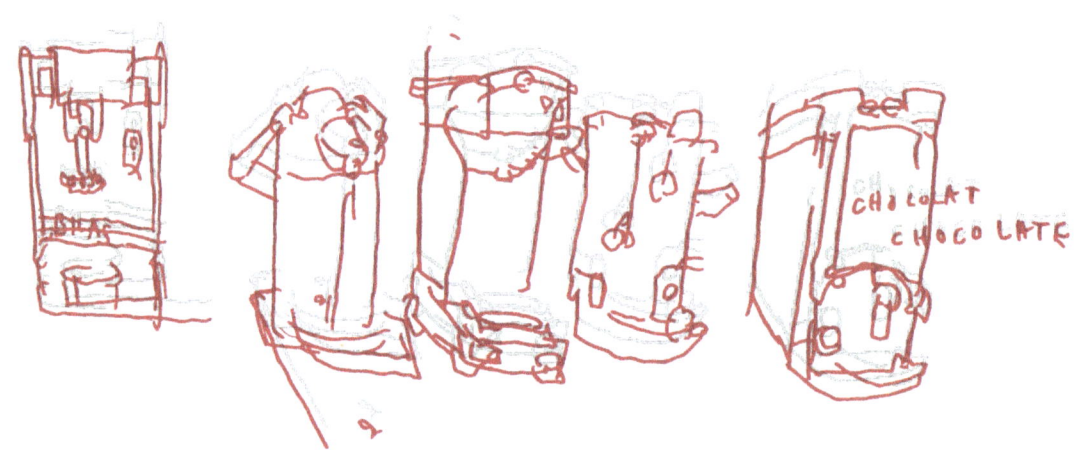

Coffee makers (pen w/ digital color) / *Paris, France*

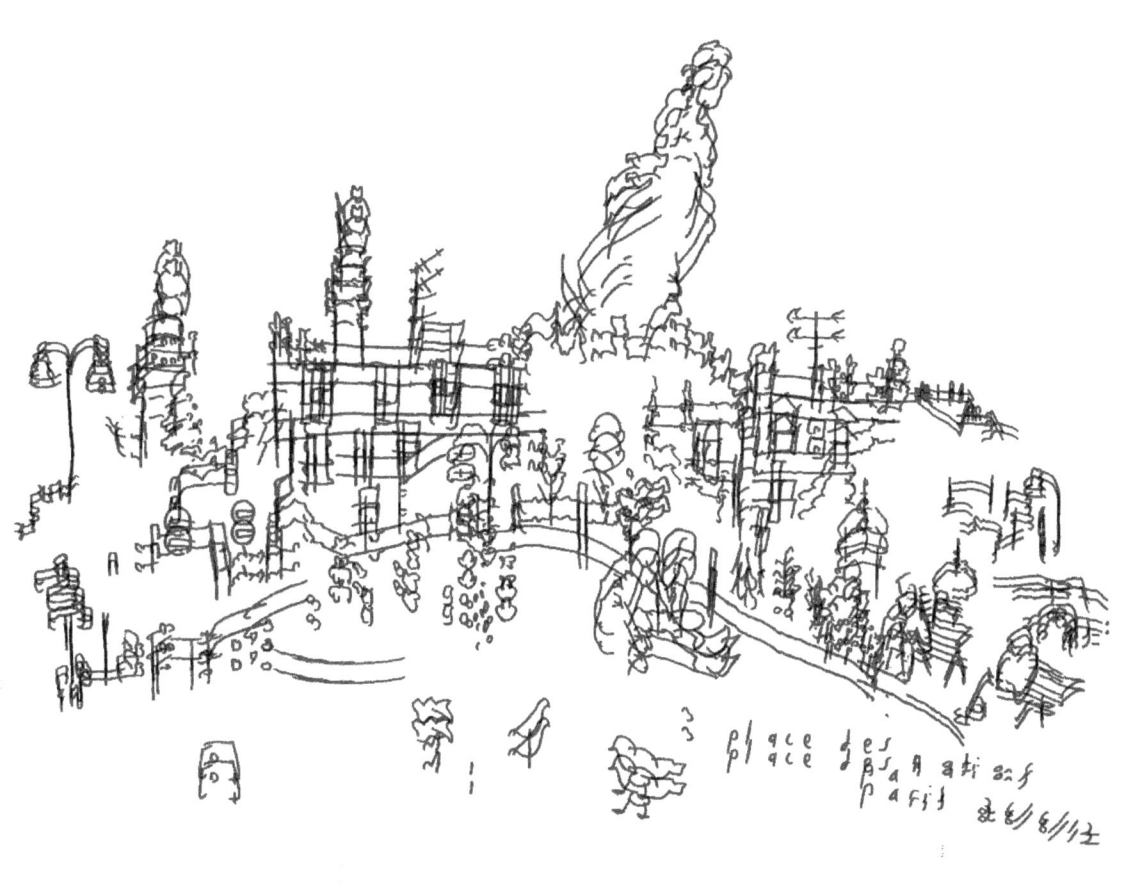

La Place de la Nation (pen) / *Paris, France*

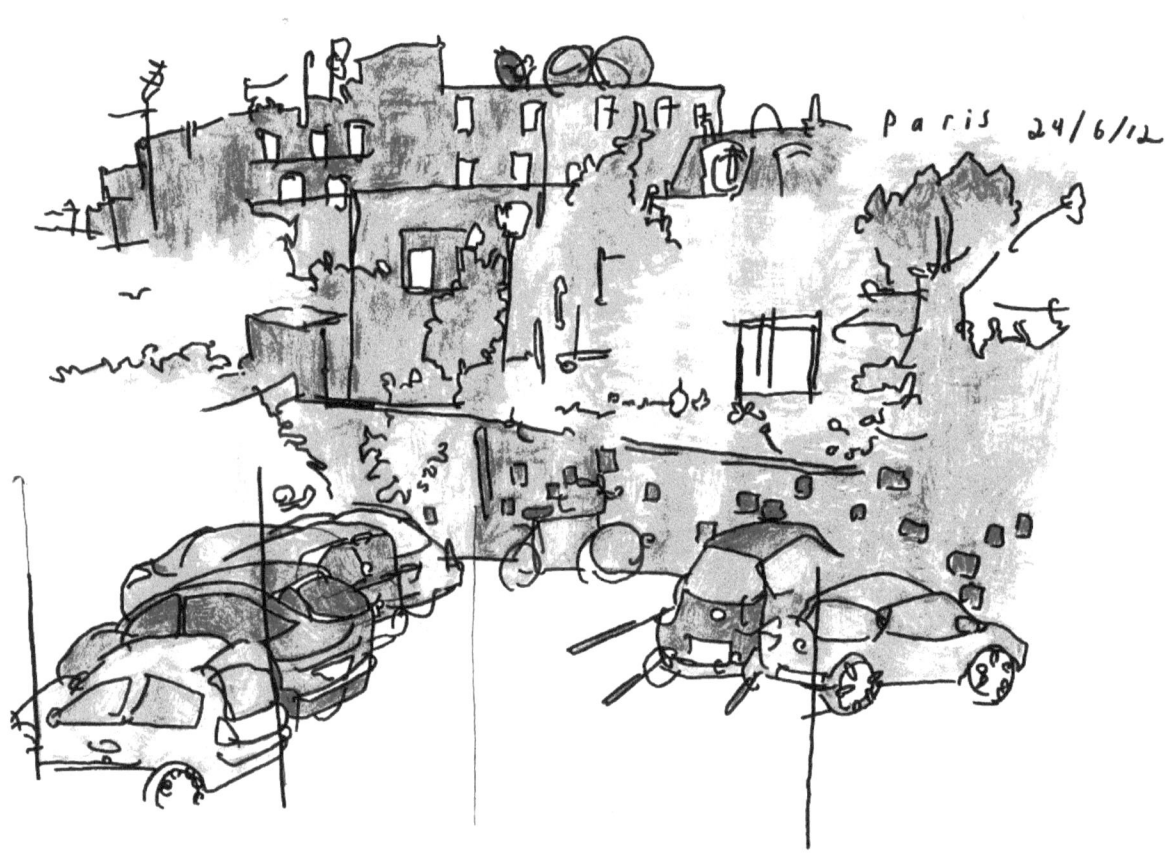

Untitled No. 1 (grayscale) / *Paris, France*

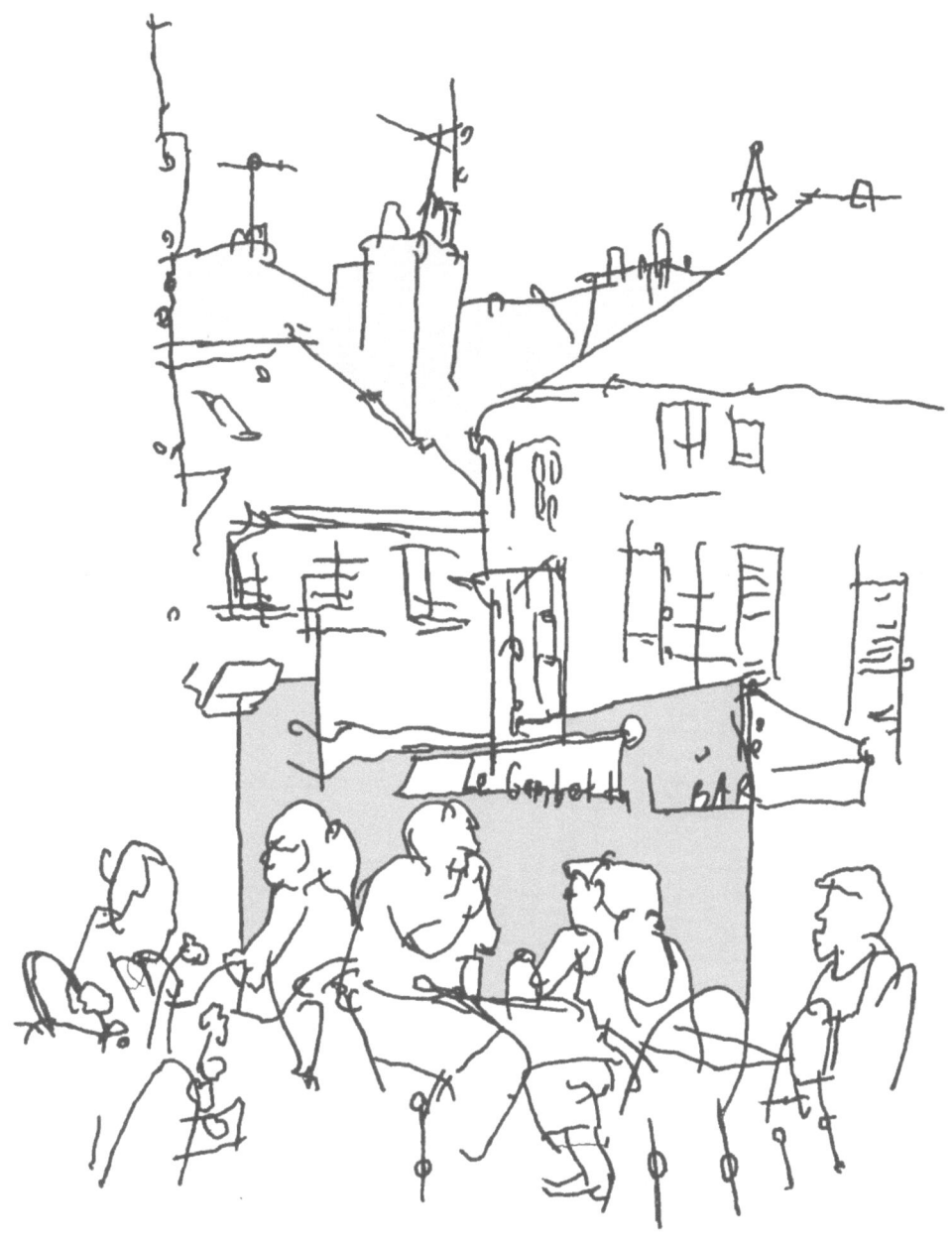

Untitled No. 1 (pen w/ digital shading) / *Poitiers, France*

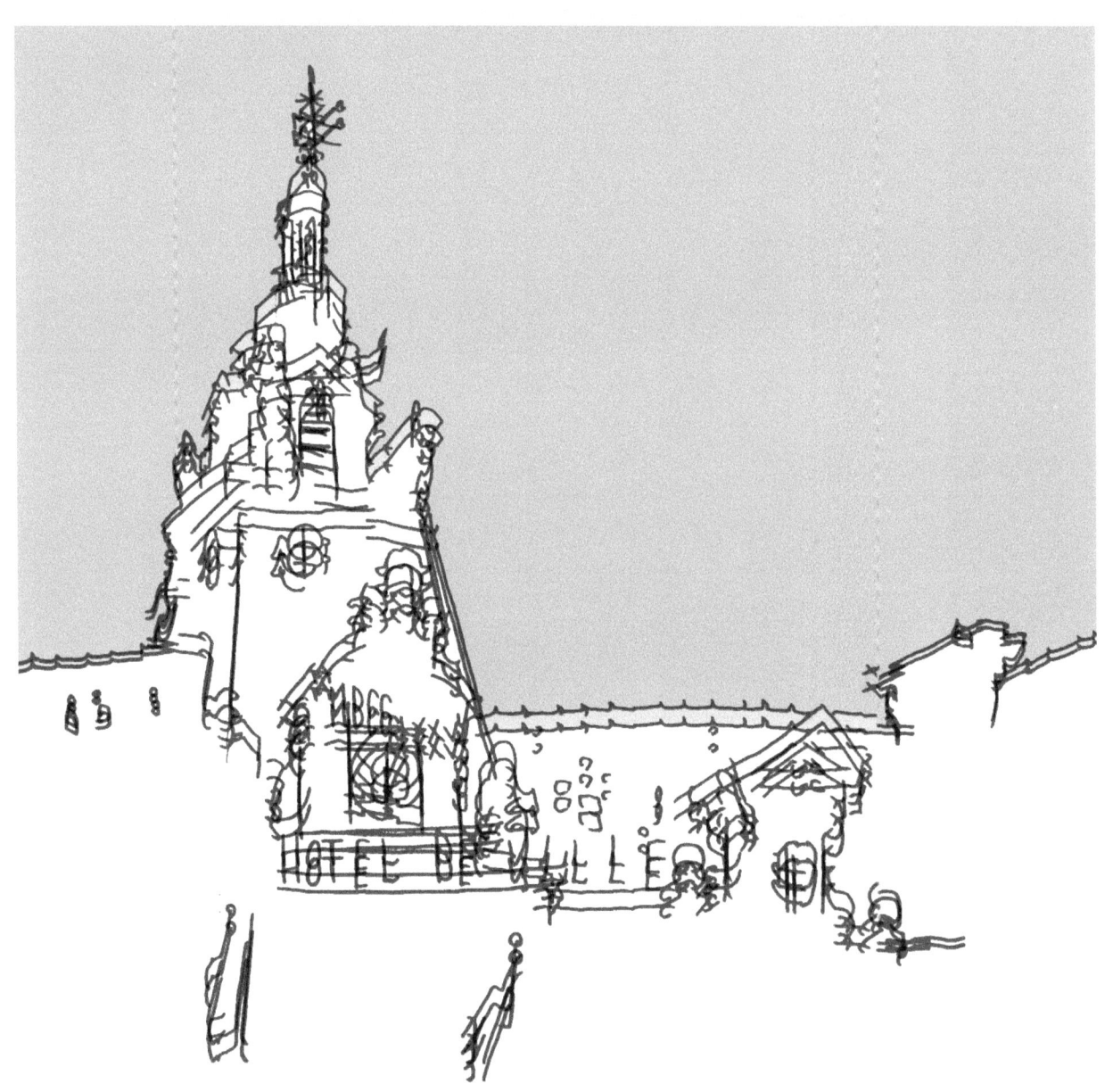

Untitled No. 2 (pen w/ digital shading) / *Poitiers, France*

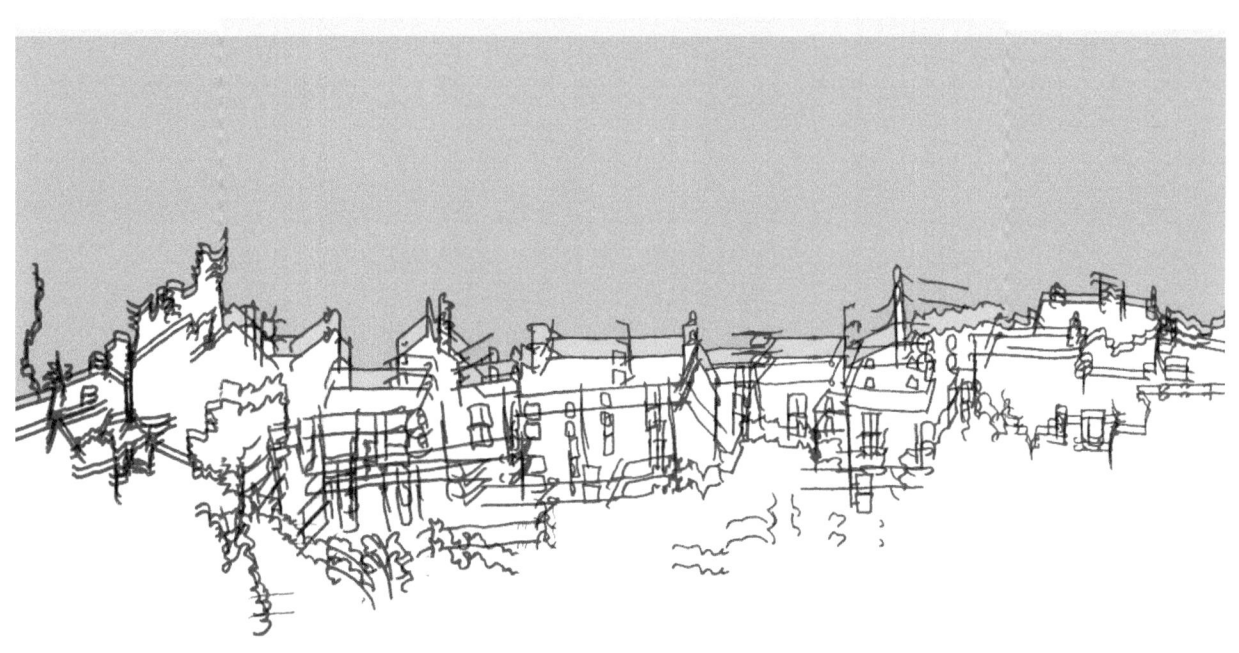

Untitled No. 3 (pen w/ digital shading) / *Poitiers, France*

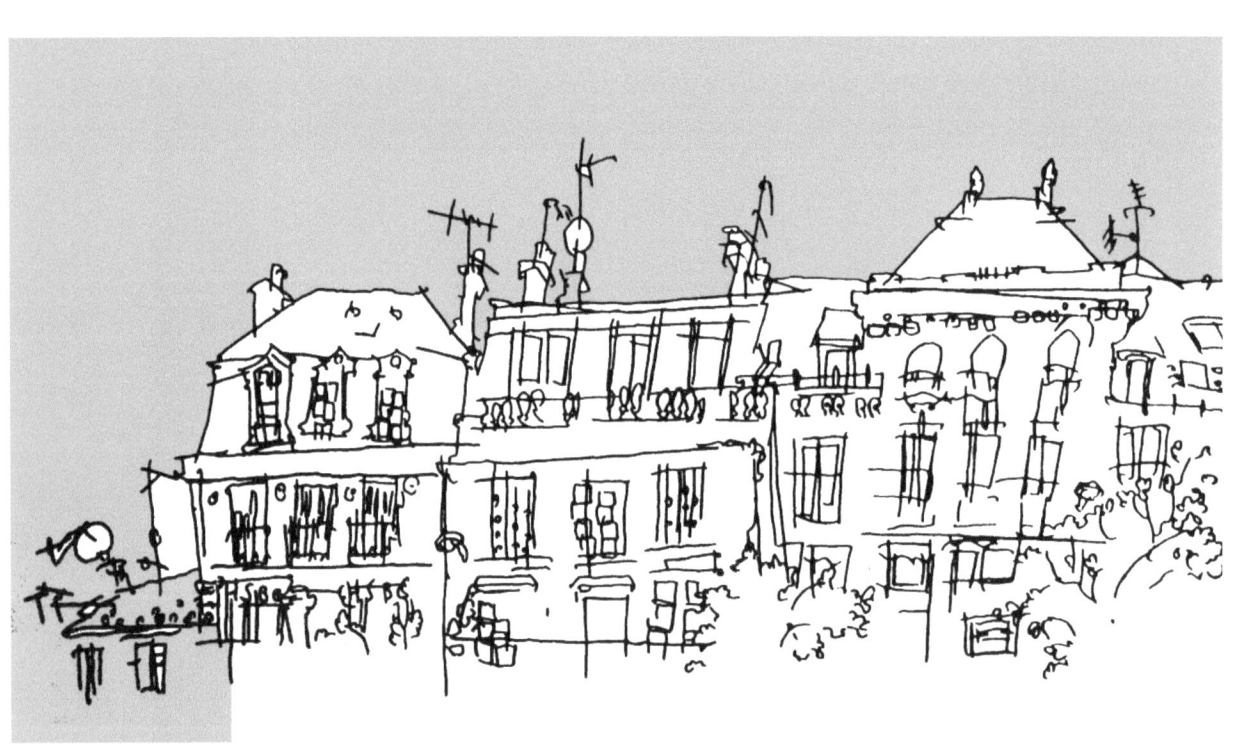

Untitled No. 4 (pen w/ digital shading) / *Poitiers, France*

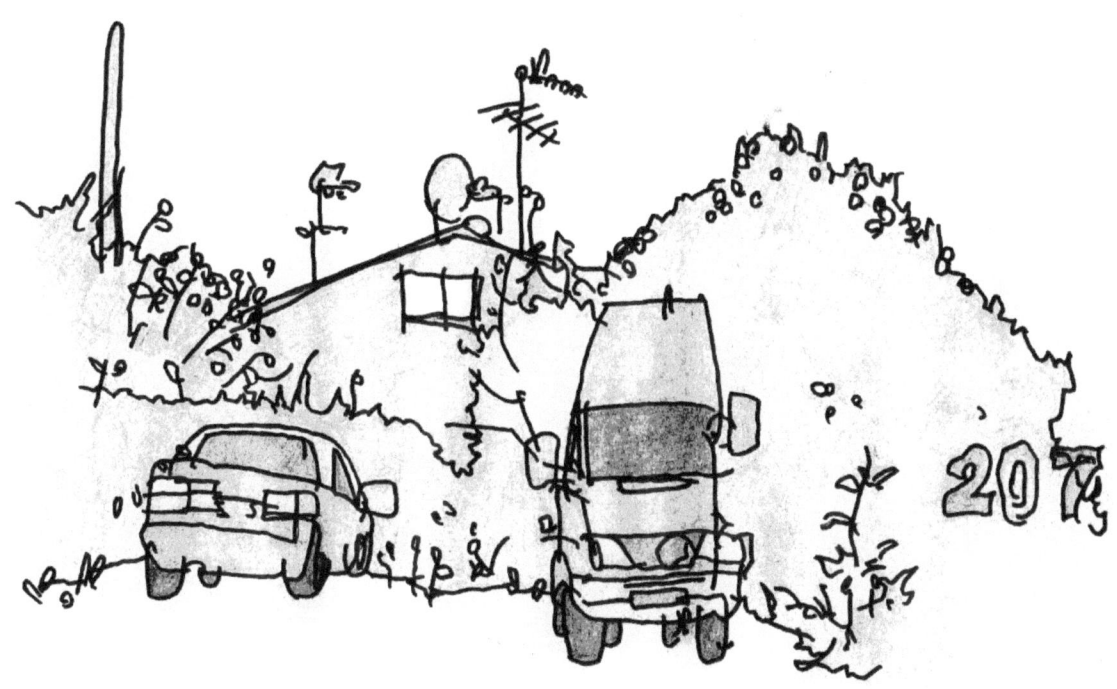

Untitled No. 5 (grayscale) / *Poitiers, France*

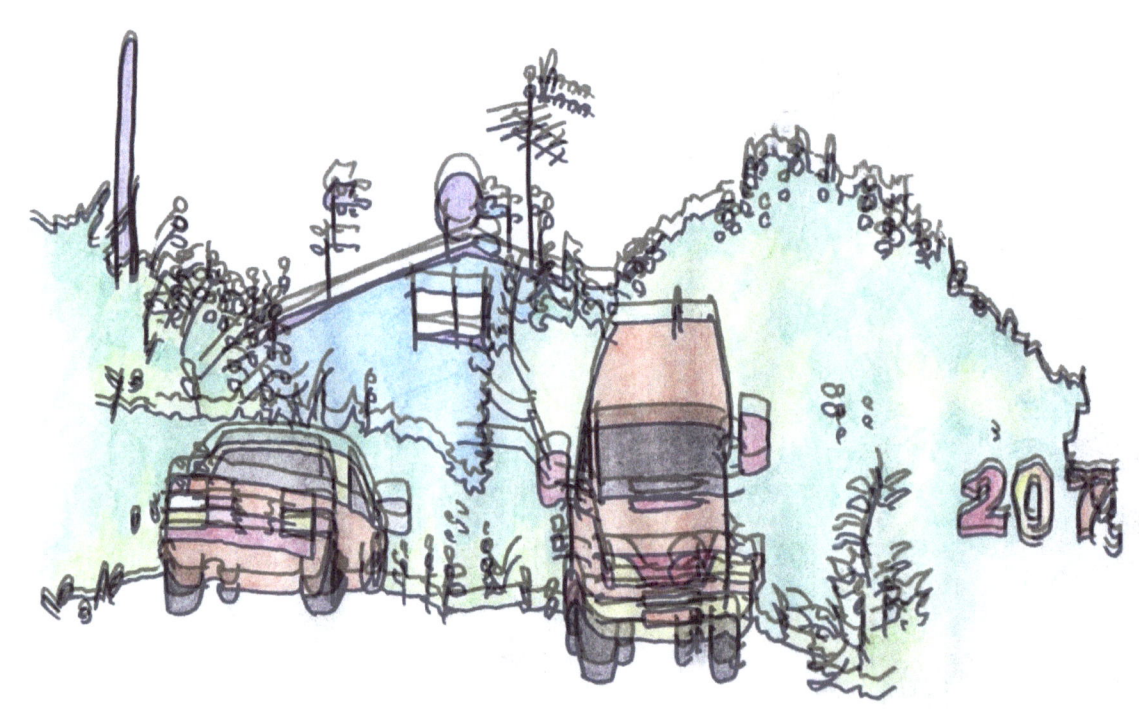

Untitled N8: 5 (pen w/ colored pencil) / *Poitiers, France*

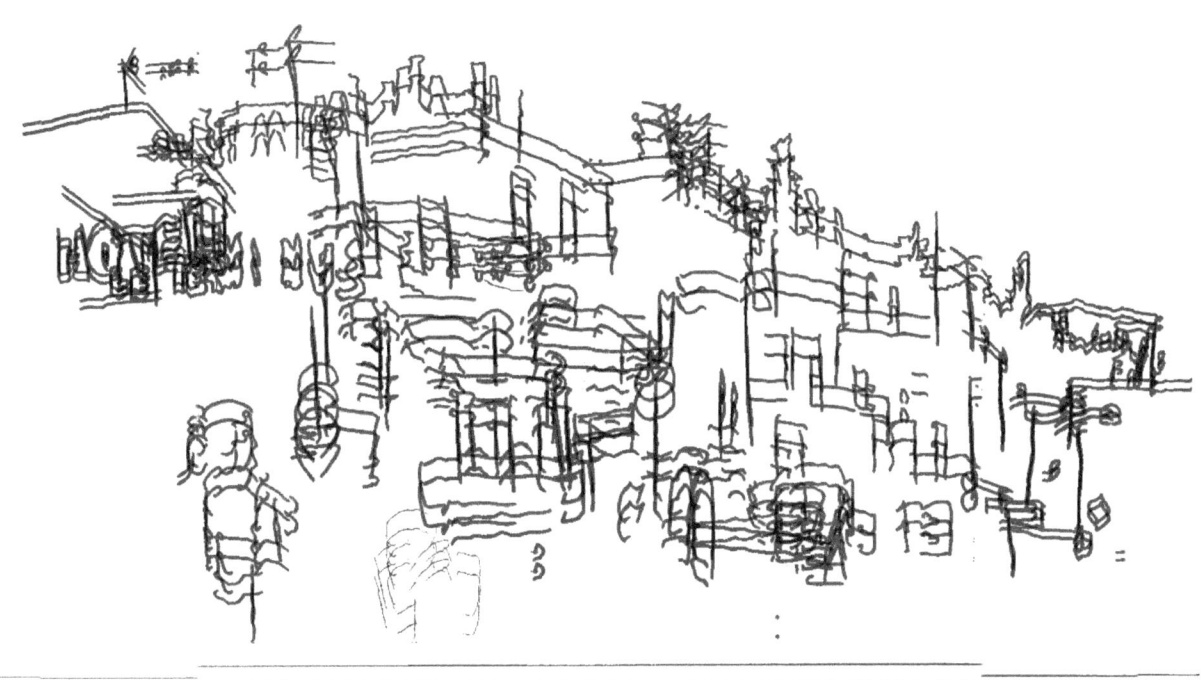

Untitled No: 6 (pen) / *Poitiers, France*

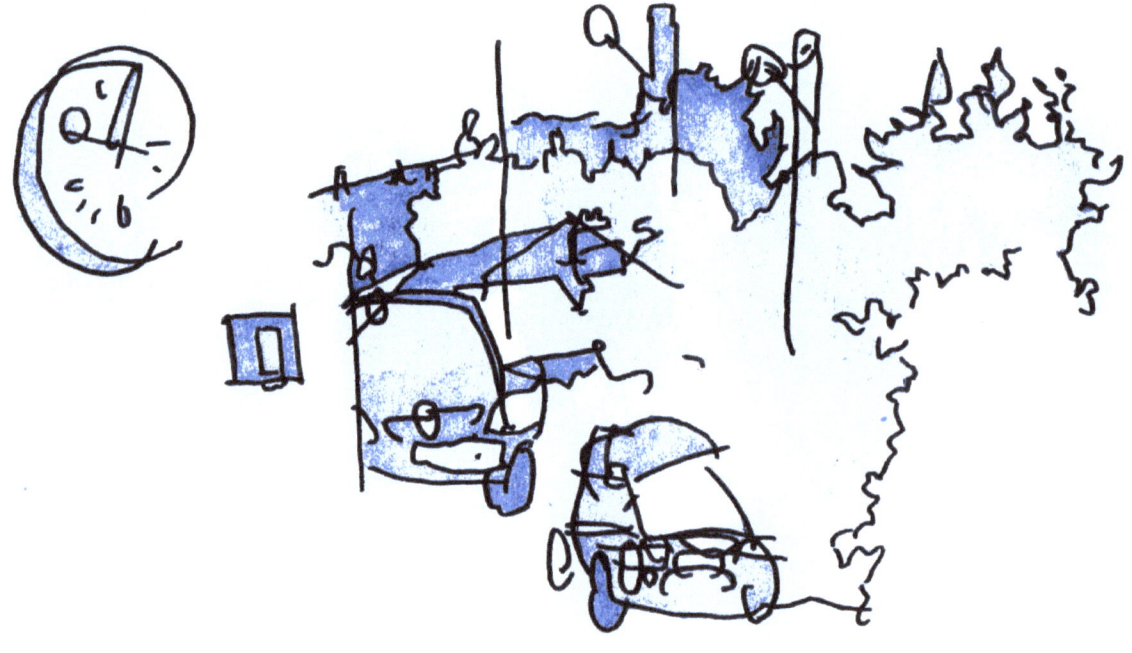

Untitled No. 7 (bluescale) / *Poitiers, France*

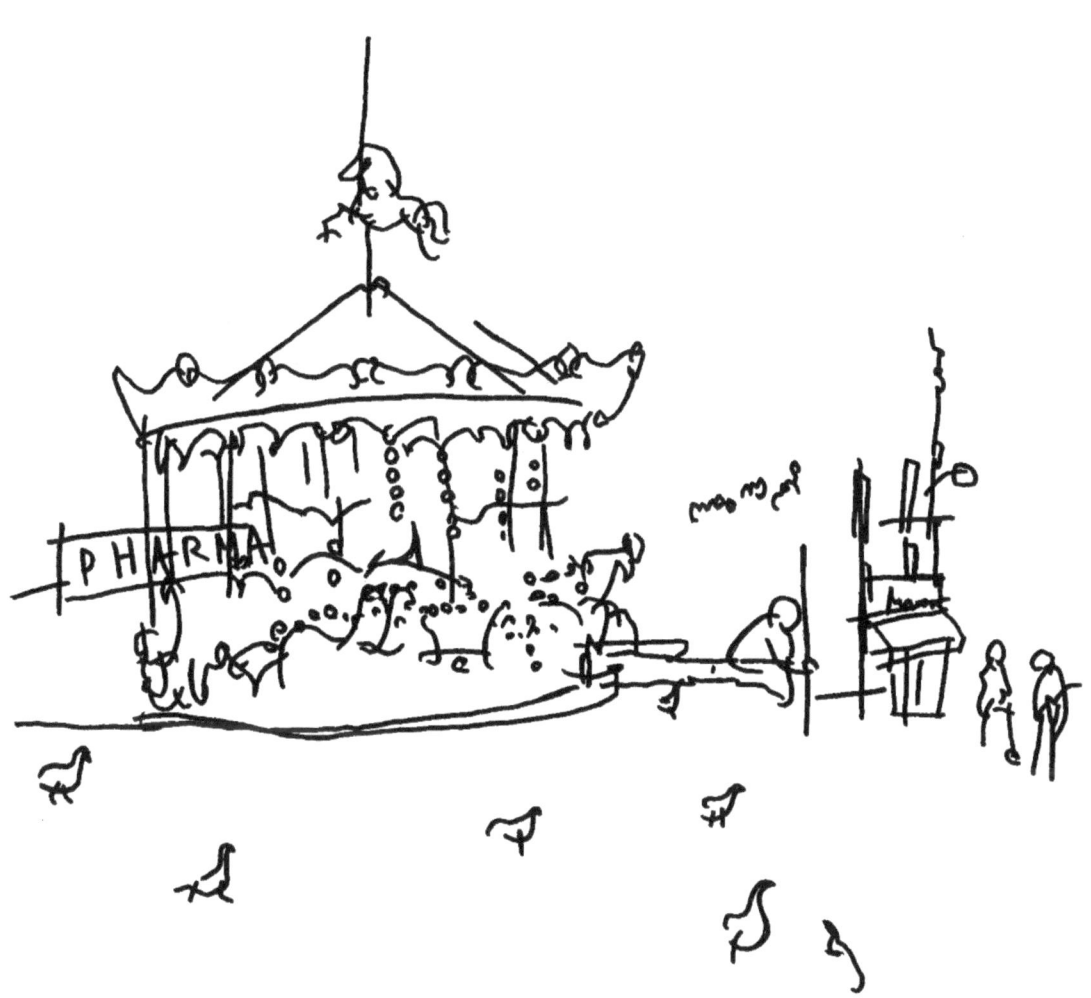

Untitled No. 8 (pen) / *Poitiers, France*

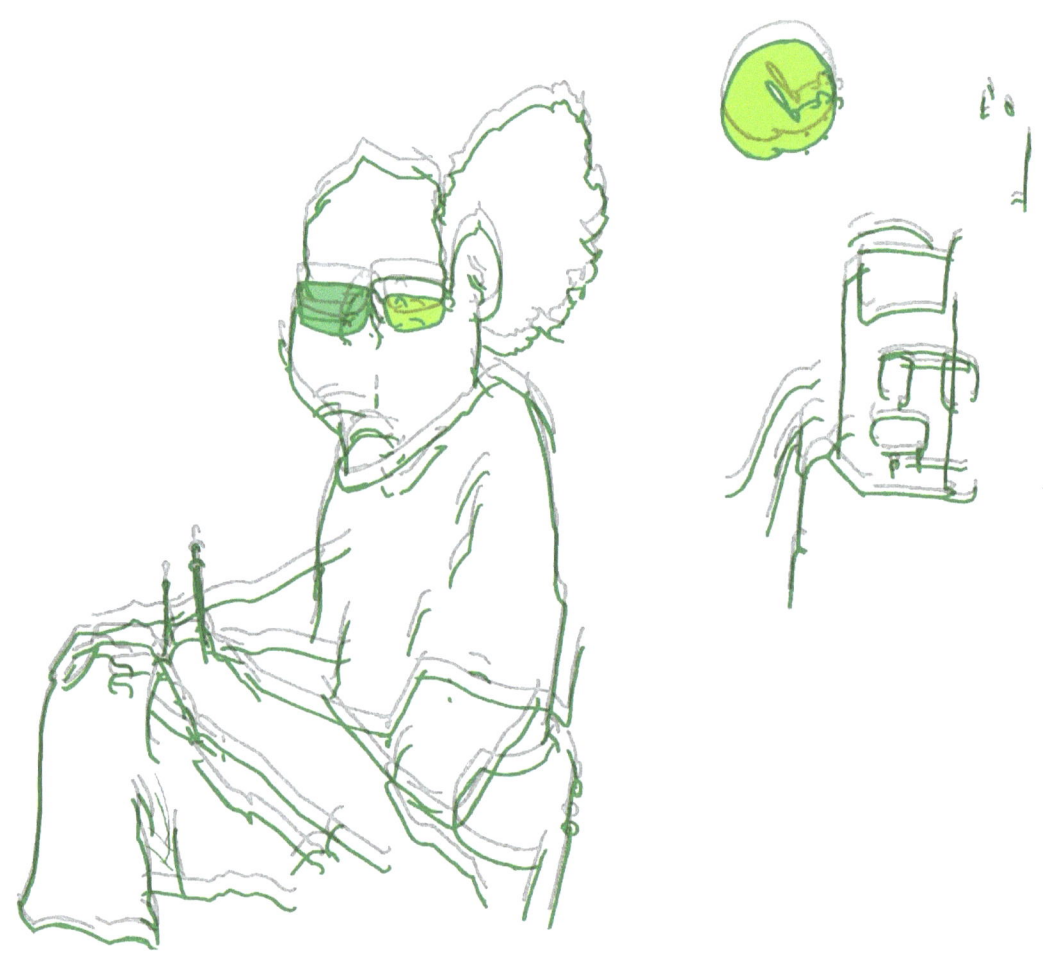

Self-portrait (pen) / *Poitiers, France*

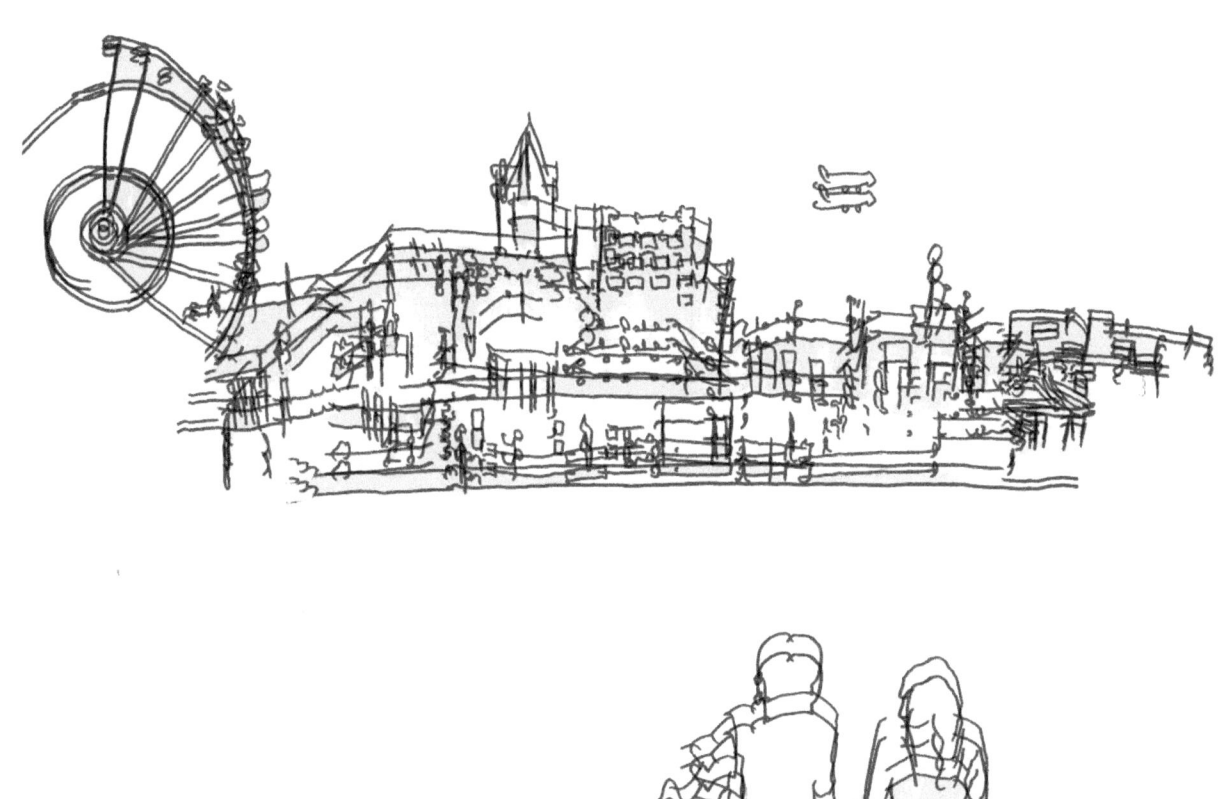

Garonne No. 1 (pen w/ digital shading) // *Toulouse, France*

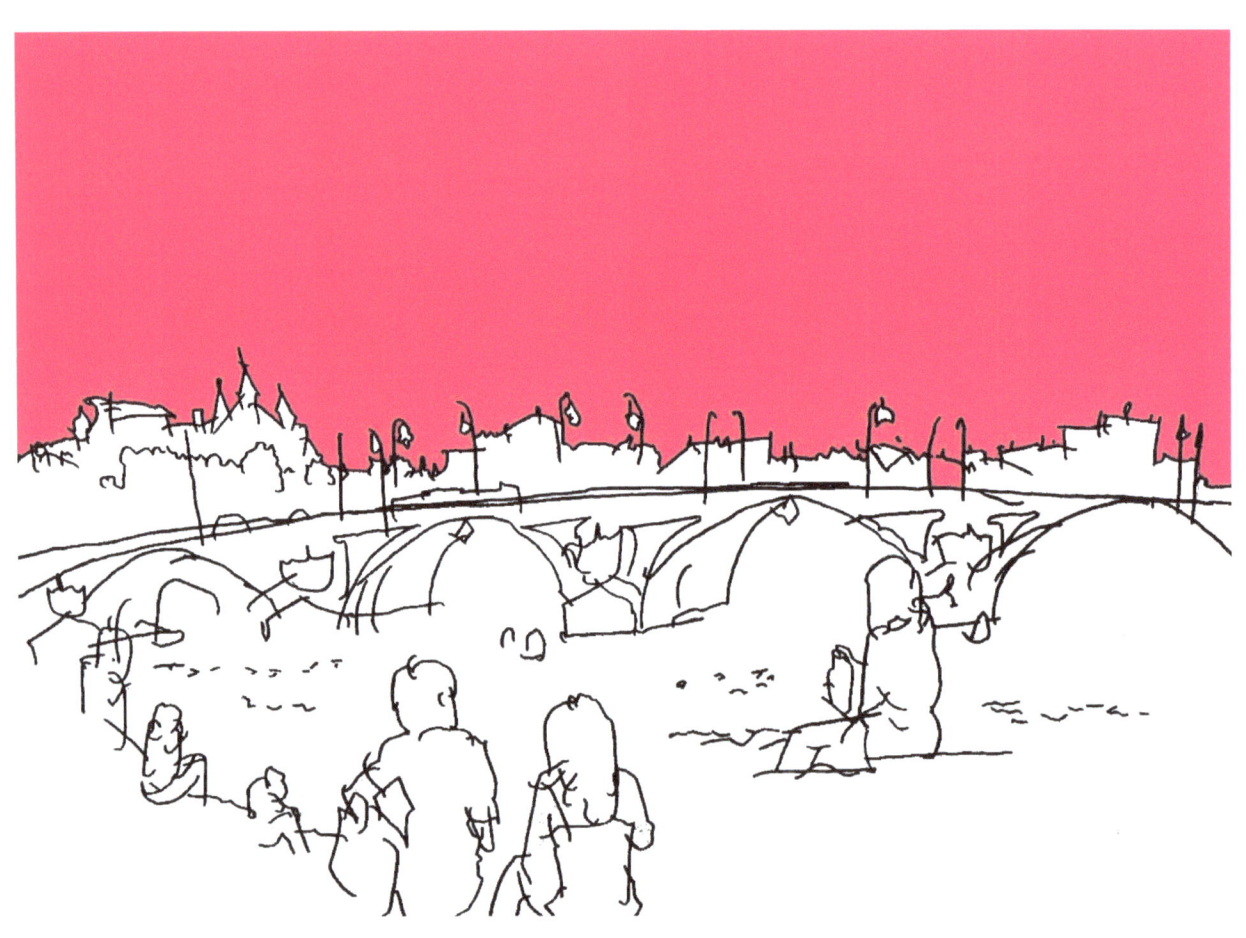

Garonne No. 2 (pen w/ digital color) / *Toulouse, France*

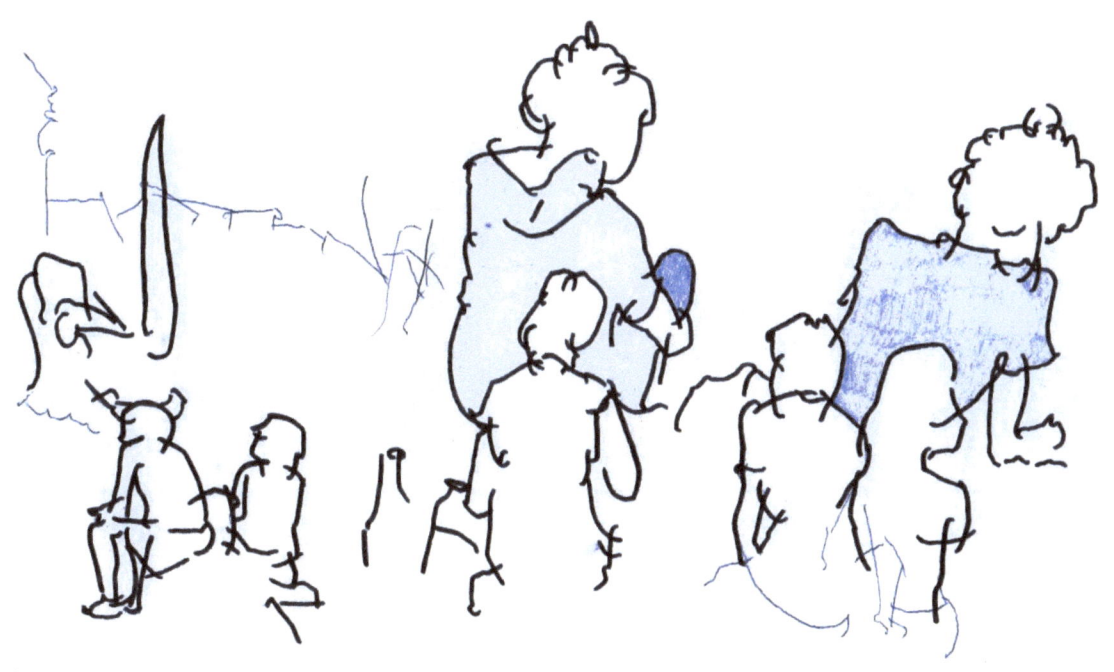

Garonne No. 3 (bluescale) / *Toulouse, France*

"Twenty years from now you will be more disappointed by the things that you didn't do than by the ones you did do. So throw off the bowlines. Sail away from the safe harbor. Catch the trade winds in your sails. Explore. Dream. Discover."

= Mark Twain

www.ingramcontent.com/pod-product-compliance
Lightning Source LLC
Chambersburg PA
CBHW051937210526
45473CB00006B/2285